Asian Animals
Giant Pandas

by Lyn A. Sirota

Consulting Editor: Gail Saunders-Smith, PhD

Content Consultant: Tanya Dewey, PhD
University of Michigan Museum of Zoology

CAPSTONE PRESS
a capstone imprint

Pebble Plus is published by Capstone Press,
151 Good Counsel Drive, P.O. Box 669, Mankato, Minnesota 56002.
www.capstonepress.com

092009
005618CGS10

Library of Congress Cataloging-in-Publication Data
Sirota, Lyn A., 1963–
    Giant pandas / by Lyn A. Sirota.
    p. cm. — (Pebble plus. Asian animals)
    Summary: "Simple text and photographs present giant pandas, how they look, where they live, and what
they do" — Provided by publisher.
    Includes bibliographical references and index.
    ISBN 978-1-4296-4028-2 (library binding)
    ISBN 978-1-4296-4845-5 (paperback)
    1. Giant panda — Juvenile literature. I. Title.
QL737.C214S4512 2010
599.789 — dc22   2009028642

Editorial Credits
Katy Kudela, editor; Matt Bruning, designer; Svetlana Zhurkin, media researcher; Eric Manske, production specialist

Photo Credits
Alamy/Mike Hill, 15; Alamy/Robert Harding Picture Library, 13; Alamy/Verge Images, 9; Corbis/Keren Su, 7; Getty
Images/National Geographic/Taylor S. Kennedy, 11; iStockphoto/Sam Lee, 1; Minden Pictures/Katherine Feng, 19;
Peter Arnold/Biosphoto/J.-L. Klein & M.-L. Hubert, cover; Photolibrary/Mike Powles, 17; Shutterstock/fenghui, 21;
Shutterstock/openbestdesignstock, 5

Note to Parents and Teachers

The Asian Animals series supports national science standards related to life science.
This book describes and illustrates giant pandas. The images support early readers in
understanding the text. The repetition of words and phrases helps early readers learn new
words. This book also introduces early readers to subject-specific vocabulary words, which are
defined in the Glossary section. Early readers may need assistance to read some words and to
use the Table of Contents, Glossary, Read More, Internet Sites, and Index sections of the book.

Table of Contents

Living in Asia

Giant pandas live

in China's bamboo forests.

They sit and munch

on bamboo all day.

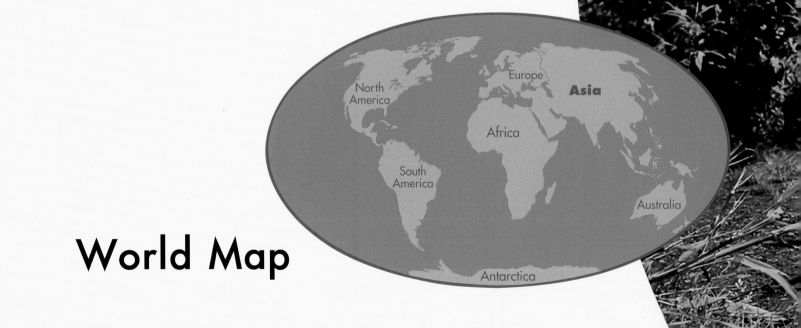

World Map

Giant pandas make their home
only in central China.
These bears live alone,
except for mothers
raising cubs.

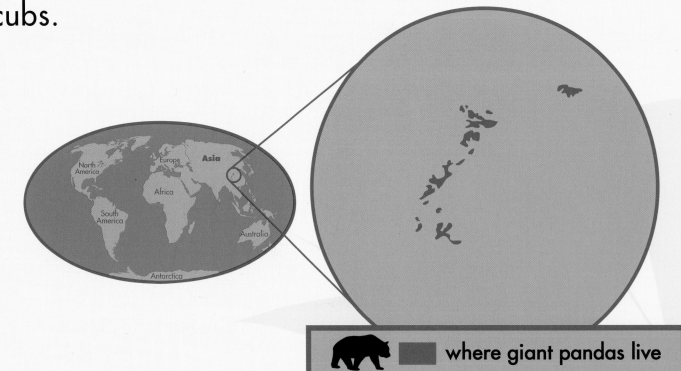

where giant pandas live

Up Close!

Giant pandas are white bears.

They have black fur

around their eyes, ears,

chest, and legs.

Pandas have four paws
with five sharp claws.
A bone in their front paws
acts like a thumb.
It helps pandas hold bamboo.

Pandas peel bamboo
with their wide teeth.
Crush!
Their strong jaws break
bamboo into pieces.

Eating and Drinking

Pandas' main meal is bamboo.
These big bears also snack
on grass, fruit, and
small animals.

Pandas get water

from the bamboo they eat.

They also drink water

from mountain streams.

Staying Safe

Panda cubs are born helpless.

Cubs stay with their mothers

for up to two years.

Mothers teach them

to find food and climb trees.

Pandas are endangered.
They are losing their land
to cities and farms.
People are working to give
pandas safe places to live.

Glossary

bamboo — a kind of tall grass with a tough stem

claw — a hard, curved nail on the feet of some animals

cub — a young panda bear

endangered — in danger of dying out

jaw — a part of the mouth used to grab, bite, and chew

peel — to remove or to pull off; a panda peels off the hard outside layer of bamboo.

Read More

Cruickshank, Don. *Giant Pandas.* Amazing Animals. New York: Weigl Publishers, 2007.

Levine, Michelle. *Giant Pandas.* Animals. Minneapolis: Lerner, 2006.

Spilsbury, Louise, and Richard Spilsbury. *Giant Panda.* Save Our Animals! Chicago: Heinemann Library, 2006.

Internet Sites

FactHound offers a safe, fun way to find Internet sites related to this book. All of the sites on FactHound have been researched by our staff.

Here's all you do:

Visit *www.facthound.com*

FactHound will fetch the best sites for you!

Index

Word Count: 164
Grade: 1
Early-Intervention Level: 18